D1166227

# DESIGN &
# DESTROY

Brimming with creative inspiration, how-to projects, and useful information to enrich your everyday life, Quarto Knows is a favorite destination for those pursuing their interests and passions. Visit our site and dig deeper with our books into your area of interest: Quarto Creates, Quarto Cooks, Quarto Homes, Quarto Lives, Quarto Drives, Quarto Explores, Quarto Gifts, or Quarto Kids.

First published in 2021 by Chartwell Books, an imprint of The Quarto Group,
142 West 36th Street, 4th Floor, New York, NY 10018, USA
T (212) 779-4972  F (212) 779-6058  www.QuartoKnows.com

Chartwell titles are also available at discount for retail, wholesale, promotional, and bulk purchase. For details, contact the Special Sales Manager by email at specialsales@quarto.com or by mail at The Quarto Group, Attn: Special Sales Manager, 100 Cummings Center Suite 265D, Beverly, MA 01915 USA.

10 9 8 7 6 5 4 3 2 1

ISBN: 978-0-7858-3930-9

Publisher: Rage Kindelsperger
Creative Director: Laura Drew
Managing Editor: Cara Donaldson
Project Editor: Leeann Moreau
Illustrator: Lilly Drew
Cover Design: Laura Drew

Printed in China

# DESIGN &
# DESTROY

Draw, Paint, Rip,
and Ruin This Book

Lilly Drew

chartwell
books

Every act of creation is first
an act of destruction.

-PABLO PICASSO

The beautiful thing about art is that there is always something to do. Creating art can come from both the building and the destruction of things. Each prompt within these pages provides a unique opportunity to use your artistic skills in unusual ways to produce something beautiful that you might not have thought to create on your own. You can find creativity in the simplest things. Let your imagination run wild on each and every page—filling it with an explosion of different art materials and colors.

Just remember that each prompt can harness your own individual style. Art is a complete spectrum, and there is something for everyone, so keep that in mind, and know that there are no rules.

This journal is meant to channel and express your creativity. It's designed to help you through any type of creative block. Use it to work through ideas and experiment with new ways you can expand your horizons. It is a private space where you can draw, write, and create—it can be a cathartic experience to those who need it. As you complete this journal, make sure to keep an open mind and—most importantly—have fun!

CREATE AN
IMAGE USING
COFFEE

SEW A BUTTON
ON TO
THE PAGE

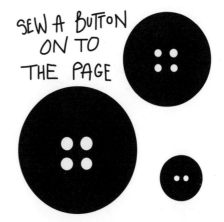

CREATE A
MOVIE
POSTER
FROM
MAGAZINES

PRESS
FLOWERS
ONTO
THE
PAGE

THE
LEFT
SIDE
OF
THE
BRAIN

THE RIGHT SIDE OF THE BRAIN

SMUDGE the page with your FINGER PRINTS

CRUMPLE
UP THIS
PAGE

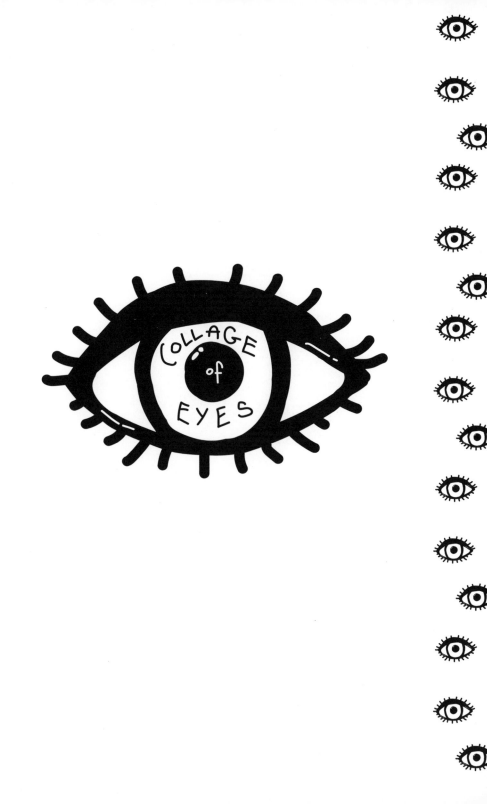

Fill the page with SPLATTERPAINT

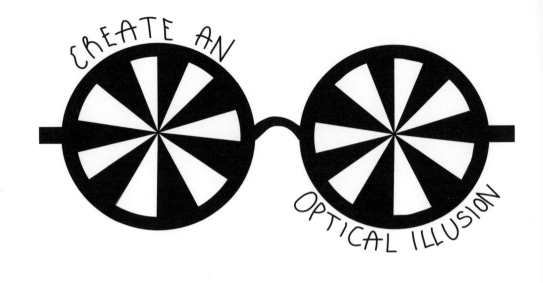
CREATE AN OPTICAL ILLUSION

MAKE A PAPER CRANE
FROM THIS PAGE

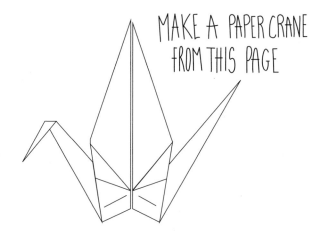

DRAW YOUR CURRENT MOOD

# Tic-Tac-Toe Page

make your own
genie
& write your
wishes

crack the spine of the book

create
a
Look
for
the
MET
GALA

PASTA THE
PAGE

DRAW
IN THE CIRCLE
UNTIL
THE PAGE
RIPS

# THROUGH THE LENS OF A KALIDOSCOPE

BUBBLES PAGE

practice
your
signature

CREATE A
DYSTOPIAN
LANDSCAPE

create
a party
for a special
event

CONNECT the
DOTs with String

WRITE YOUR FAVORITE SONG LYRICS

USE
ALL
YOUR
ART
SUPPLIES
ON
THE
PAGE

CREATE AN
ALIEN
AND
THEIR
SPACESHIP

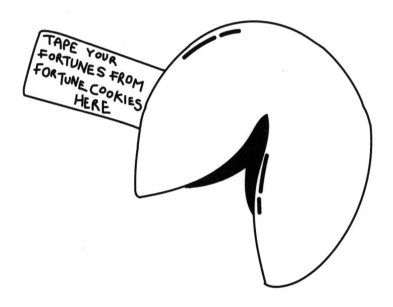

TAPE YOUR
FORTUNES FROM
FORTUNE COOKIES
HERE

CREATE A MANDALA ON THIS PAGE

DRAW
YOUR HOUSE
WITHOUT USING
ART MATERIALS

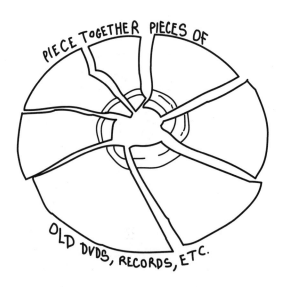

PIECE TOGETHER PIECES OF OLD DVDS, RECORDS, ETC.

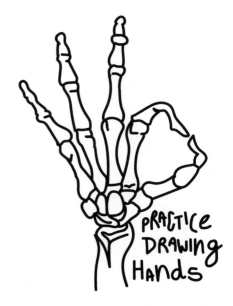

PRACTICE
DRAWING
HANDS

TYE DYE

THIS PAGE

page of
silver

page of gold

# Dream Vacation Itinerary

create a
fruit bowl out
of magazine
pictures

CREATE AN
INESCAPABLE
MAZE

DRAW your PHONE SCREEN

STRESS RELIEF PAGE

DRAW THINGS THAT MAKE YOU CALM

# PLACE LEAVES

# CHANGING COLOR HERE

WRITE A
HAIKU

TRACE
STONES
& SHELLS
YOU FIND
HERE

CREATE BLIND CONTOUR SKETCHES

# CONDIMENT LOG

|  |  |  |
|--|--|--|
|  |  |  |
|  |  |  |
|  |  |  |

DRAW USING
WHITE ART MATERIALS

SMEAR GRAPHITE ONTO THE PAGE

MAKE A BLACKOUT POEM FROM A PAGE OF YOUR FAVORITE BOOK

DRAW WHAT IS IN YOUR BAG

DESCRIBE A COLOR AS IF YOU WERE SPEAKING
TO SOMEONE WHO IS UNABLE TO SEE IT

PASTE BIRD FEATHERS ON THIS PAGE

DESIGN A FAIRGROUND
RIDE ON THE PAGE

DRAW YOUR FAMILY CREST

Nonstop Line
Covering the
Page

PASTE
YOUR FAVORITE
IMAGE
HERE

PASTE A
FOUR-LEAF
CLOVER
ON THE PAGE

RUB FOODY FINGERS ON THE PAGE

PLACE WRAPPERS FROM FOOD YOU EAT OFTEN COVERING THE PAGE

DRAW A SCENE FROM A FAIRY TALE

WRITE DOWN YOUR GOALS

DRAW OR WRITE YOUR FAVORITE HOLIDAY MEMORY

CREATE
A DRAGON
AND THEIR EGG

MELT AN ICECUBE
ON THIS PAGE

SOMEONE WHO INSPIRES YOU

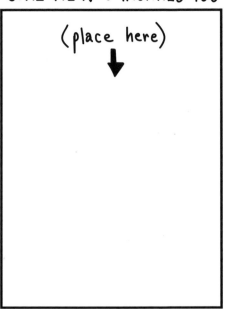

(place here)

↓

DRAW HOW THEY MAKE YOU FEEL

WRITE A
WORD
TO DESCRIBE
EVERY DAY
UNTIL THE
PAGE IS FULL

FRINGE
THE PAGE

CREATE A STORM

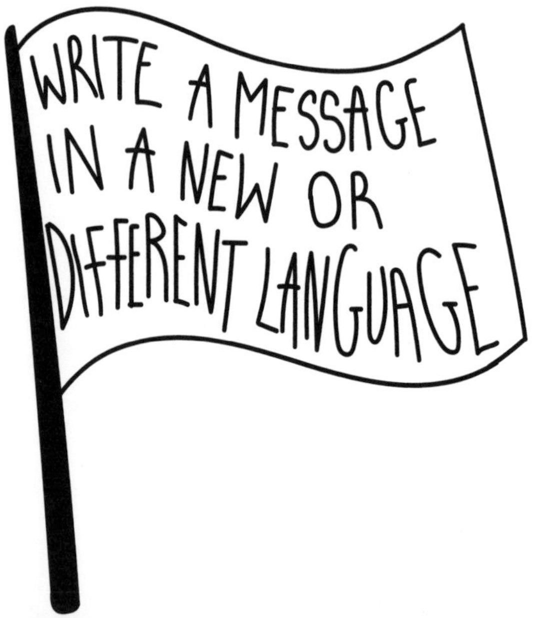

WRITE A MESSAGE
IN A NEW OR
DIFFERENT LANGUAGE

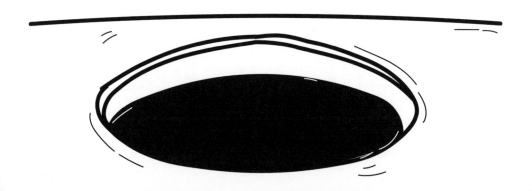

 CREATE A
SCENIC ENVIRONMENT
OUT OF GARBAGE

TEST YOUR
NEW & OLD MARKERS
ON THIS PAGE

MAKE YOUR OWN MEME

WRITE MEMORABLE BOOK/TV/MOVIE QUOTES

WIPE MAKEUP ONTO THE PAGE

CREATE A

MONSTER UNDER THE
BED

CREATE A
MOOD BOARD

TEAR OUT A HEADLINE
FROM A NEWSPAPER
AND DRAW A PICTURE
TO GO WITH IT

PRACTICE
WRITING/DRAWING
WITH YOUR
NONDOMINANT HAND

CREATE & DESIGN YOUR OWN WORLD MAP

# GIVE THIS PAGE
## TO SOMEONE AS A PRESENT

CAMO
THE
PAGE

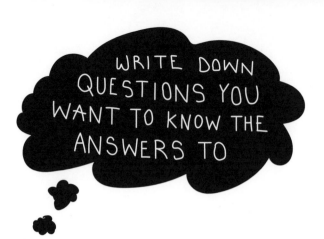

# RECEIPT

PASTE A
RECEIPT
HERE
AND DRAW
A PERSON
TO MATCH
THE ORDER

# DRAW WHAT'S RIGHT IN FRONT OF YOU WHEN YOU FLIP TO THIS PAGE

RIP THIS PAGE INTO THE SMALLEST PIECES POSSIBLE

create your own business card.

CREATE
A
MYTHICAL
CREATURE
PARK

WRITE A
SELF-LOVE
LETTER
TO YOURSELF

WATER COLOR PRACTICE PAGE

DRAW THE
SMALL THINGS
THAT MAKE
YOU HAPPY

SET/SPILL YOUR DRINK HERE

PASTE AN OLD ARTWORK HERE AND REDRAW IT ON THE NEXT PAGE

CREATE A RAINBOW

RUN THIS PAGE OVER

DRAW
A CLOCK
AND LABEL THE TIME
WHEN YOU
FINISH
THE
PIECE

PLACE STICKERS ON THE PAGE

CREATE A
STRAWBERRY
USING RED
MATERIALS

PASTE, DRAW AND WRITE THINGS THAT REMIND YOU OF SUMMER

COVER THE PAGE IN
PAGE IN

TEMPORARY TATTOOS

# TEXTURE LOG

|  |  |  |
|---|---|---|
|  |  |  |
|  |  |  |
|  |  |  |

create
a design from
sharp/textured items

Cover the Page with STAMPS

CANDY
WRAPPER
PAGE

RUN OUT
AN ENTIRE PEN
ON THE PAGE

# Write Your Favorite Word All Over The Page

CREATE A GIANT SPIRAL

# DRAW YOUR ZOMBIE SURVIVAL GUIDE KIT

CREATE A
WORD SEARCH
WITH ODD
WORDS

TAPE
THE PAGE

USING
DUCT TAPE,
WASHI TAPE,
etc.

# CREATE A ZINE

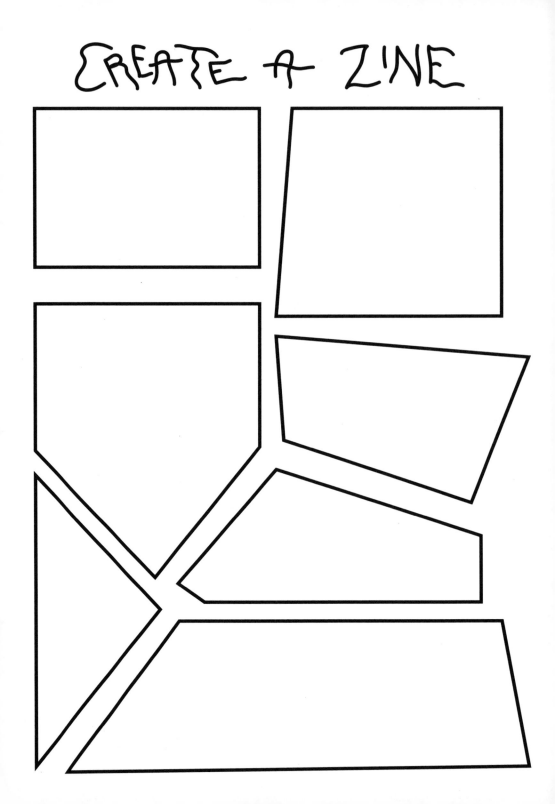

USE
THIS
PAGE
AS A
SHOPPING
LIST

SOAP

WASH THE PAGE

CREATE A

SWEET
GINGERBREAD HOUSE

CREATE A
SECRET LETTER
& TEAR UP PAGE

DRAW AND CREATE
YOUR OWN WAND;
PASTE DOWN
MATERIALS
THAT THE
WAND WOULD
BE MADE OF

DRAW YOUR FAVORITE GAME CHARACTER OR ENVIRONMENT

# CREATE A

# RORSCHACH TEST

DRAW
YOUR
FEET

PIN A PIECE OF OLD

CLOTHING TO THE PAGE

DRAW A CITYSCAPE

WITH BLURRED VISION

DRAW PLAYING CARDS AS PEOPLE

DRAW
YOUR
IDEAL
PET

CREATE
YOUR OWN
ALBUM
COVER